If You Were an Elephant

written by
Leslie Staub

illustrated by
Richard Jones

putnam

G. P. Putnam's Sons

*For the newest member of the Curry-
Werhan herd, know that you were loved
before you even had a name—L.S.*

For Beatrice—R.J.

G. P. PUTNAM'S SONS

An imprint of Penguin Random House LLC, New York

G. P. Putnam's Sons is a registered trademark of
Penguin Random House LLC.

Visit us online at penguinrandomhouse.com

Library of Congress Cataloging-in-Publication Data
Names: Staub, Leslie, 1957- author. | Jones, Richard, illustrator.
Title: If you were an elephant / by Leslie Staub ;
illustrated by Richard Jones.
Description: New York, NY : G. P. Putnam's Sons, [2021]
Summary: "A factual depiction of a young African
elephant's day in the wild"—Provided by publisher.
Identifiers: LCCN 2017038283 | ISBN 9781524741341 (hc) |
ISBN 9781524741358 (epub fixed) |
ISBN 9781524741372 (kf8/Kindle) |
Subjects: LCSH: Elephants—Juvenile fiction. |
CYAC: Elephants—Fiction.
Classification: LCC PZ10.3.S7855 If 2020 | DDC [E]—dc23
LC record available at https://lccn.loc.gov/2017038283

Manufactured in China
ISBN 9781524741341
10 9 8 7 6 5 4 3 2 1

Design by Dave Kopka and Eileen Savage
Text set in Jubilat Regular | The art was done in
paint and edited digitally.

IF YOU WERE AN ELEPHANT,
you'd be the biggest animal
who lives on the land.
You'd have ears big as tent flaps,
skin thick as blankets.
You'd turn the next page
with your trunk, not your hand.

You'd walk the savanna
on legs thick as tree trunks,
on feet flat as pancakes.

You'd roam wild open places
with zebras and aardvarks,
giraffes and impalas.

Creatures would scramble
to get out of your way!

If you were an elephant,
you'd live in a herd, not a house.
You'd spend every day
with your mom and your grandma,
your aunts and your cousins.

You'd walk strong beside them.
You'd nuzzle and guide them,
and make sure the little ones
never got lost.

If you were an elephant,
you'd eat all day long.
You'd munch leaves and grasses,
whole bushes and branches.

You'd dig roots and scrape bark
with the tips of your tusks,
and wait till baboons
dropped dessert at your feet!

And when you got thirsty,
you'd tromp to the water hole.
You'd guzzle gallons and gallons.

You'd swim and you'd paddle.
You'd use your trunk as a snorkel.

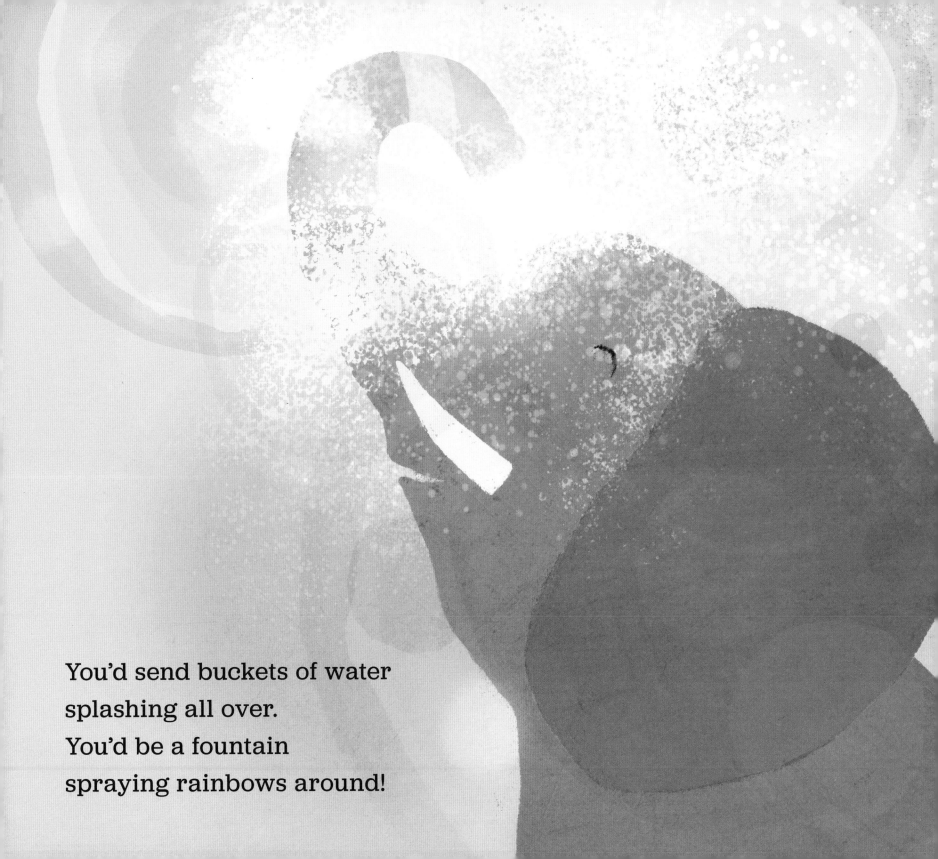

You'd send buckets of water
splashing all over.
You'd be a fountain
spraying rainbows around!

If you were an elephant,
you'd give yourself mud baths.
You'd slide and you'd roll
and throw dirt all over
until you were covered
from your trunk to your tail.

If you were an elephant
on a hot afternoon,
you'd make a breeze with your ears
to cool yourself down.

You'd nap in the shade
of an umbrella tree,
listening with your feet
to the beat of the land.

But when you sensed danger,
you'd charge and you'd thunder,
tusks flashing fiercely,
as bright as the sun.

You'd stomp and you'd trumpet.
You'd drum out a warning
that would carry a message
for miles through the ground!

When the danger was over,
you'd reach out your trunk
to the old and the young ones.
You'd touch and you'd soothe them.
You'd check them all over.
You'd let them know softly
that things are okay!

If you were an elephant,
you'd always remember
the best places to go.

And when you crossed paths
with a herd of old friends . . .

You'd rush out to greet them.
You'd call and you'd rumble.
You'd play and you'd wrestle,

until it was time
to go your own ways.

If you were an elephant
with your herd all around you,
you'd fall asleep nestled
in a pool of cool moonlight,

listening quietly . . . quietly . . .
to the song of the land.

AMAZING FACTS *about* ELEPHANTS

- **The elephants in this book are African bush elephants,** the largest of all the elephant species in the world. African bush elephants stand ten to thirteen feet tall. The biggest one ever recorded weighed over 16,000 pounds. That's as much as a small school bus!

- **Herds usually have around ten elephants, but can have as many as forty.** Elephant herds are always led by a female, called the matriarch. She is usually the oldest elephant in the group. Most members of the herd are female because when males grow up, they leave the herd and hang around by themselves or with other males.

- **Elephants spend up to sixteen hours a day eating.** They eat up to six hundred pounds of food and can drink as much as fifty gallons of water in a day.

- **Elephants have amazing memories.** Older matriarchs have the most successful herds because they remember all the places where they've found food and water during their long lives. In times of extreme drought, they lead their herds to distant water holes they remember from past droughts many years earlier.

- **Elephants are very emotional, intelligent, and caring.** They play and show joy. They express love and tenderness, sadness and concern. They even seem to cry.

- **Elephants don't just trumpet.** They also communicate by barking, snorting, roaring, rumbling, and even purring! Some of the sounds elephants make are infrasonic—too low for humans to hear.

- **Elephants listen with their ears and their feet.** They can pick up sound vibrations from many miles away—both those that travel through the air and also those that travel through the ground, which elephants can detect through the soles of their feet.

- **Though elephant skin is wrinkly and up to one inch thick on parts of their bodies,** it is sensitive enough to feel a fly and can get sunburned. Elephant moms like it when their kids take mud baths, because it helps them stay cool and because elephants use dirt as sunscreen.

- **Elephant trunks have 40,000 muscles in them.** They are strong enough to uproot a tree and coordinated enough to pick a single blade of grass.

- **Elephants are super-smellers.** They have tons of scent receptors in their extra-long noses that help them smell food and water from several miles away.

- **Tusks are actually huge overgrown teeth that keep growing for an elephant's whole life.** Unfortunately, elephants are sometimes hunted illegally for the ivory in their tusks. Poaching, along with habitat loss, has made the African bush elephant a vulnerable species.

- **Wild elephants only sleep for about two hours a day,** usually just before sunrise and during the hottest parts of the day. Herd members often take turns sleeping to stay on the lookout for danger. Elephants can sleep standing up, but they dream only when they sleep lying down.